# YOU'RE PART OF A
# NEIGHBORHOOD COMMUNITY!

BY THERESA EMMINIZER

Gareth Stevens
PUBLISHING

Please visit our website, www.garethstevens.com. For a free color catalog of all our high-quality books, call toll free 1-800-542-2595 or fax 1-877-542-2596.

Library of Congress Cataloging-in-Publication Data

Names: Emminizer, Theresa, author.
Title: You're part of a neighborhood community! / Theresa Emminizer.
Description: New York : Gareth Stevens, [2020] | Series: All our communities
  | Includes index.
Identifiers: LCCN 2019017369| ISBN 9781538245378 (pbk.) | ISBN 9781538245392
  (library bound) | ISBN 9781538245385 (6 pack)
Subjects: LCSH: Neighborhoods–Juvenile literature. | Community
  life–Juvenile literature. | Communities–Juvenile literature.
Classification: LCC HM761 .E463 2020 | DDC 307–dc23
LC record available at https://lccn.loc.gov/2019017369

Published in 2020 by
**Gareth Stevens Publishing**
111 East 14th Street, Suite 349
New York, NY 10003

Designer: Sarah Liddell
Editor: Theresa Emminizer

Photo credits: cover, pp. 1, 7 Monkey Business Images/Shutterstock.com; background texture used throughout april70/Shutterstock.com; papercut texture used throughout Paladjai/Shutterstock.com; p. 5 JJFarq/Shutterstock.com; p. 9 John Roman Images/Shutterstock.com; p. 11 Tyler Olson/Shutterstock.com; p. 13 VGstockstudio/Shutterstock.com; pp. 15, 19 Rawpixel.com/Shutterstock.com; p. 17 Africa Studio/Shutterstock.com; p. 21 karelnoppe/Shutterstock.com.

Printed in the United States of America

Some of the images in this book illustrate individuals who are models. The depictions do not imply actual situations or events.

CPSIA compliance information: Batch #CW20GS: For further information contact Gareth Stevens, New York, New York at 1-800-542-2595.

# CONTENTS

**Boldface** words appear in the glossary.

# What Is a Neighborhood?

A neighborhood is more than just a group of houses standing side by side. It's a living community! Within a neighborhood, people work together to **achieve** common **goals**. Everyone wants the neighborhood to be clean, safe, and **productive**.

5

## Your Neighborhood Community

What does your neighborhood look like? You might live in a busy city with lots of people living near you. You might live in the country where the nearest house is about a mile away. Every neighborhood is a little bit different.

# Who's in Your Community?

Special workers like firefighters and police officers are part of your neighborhood community. So are everyday **citizens** like your next-door neighbors. Young or old, everyone has a part to play.

## Community Roles

Each person has a role, or job, within the community. Police officers make sure the neighborhood is safe. Trash **collectors** keep it clean. **Ordinary** citizens can serve the community too. They work at shops, schools, and libraries, making the neighborhood productive.

## Where Do You Fit?

Even kids have a role to play! What can you do to make your neighborhood community a better place? Think about what your neighborhood needs and what you could do to fill those needs. Talk to your family about how you can help.

# Keep It Clean

Start at home! Keep your home, yard, and street tidy. You can do this by picking up litter, raking leaves, or shoveling snow on your sidewalk. Clean homes and streets make the neighborhood look nice. You could also pick up litter at a nearby park.

# Help Out!

Think about people in your community that might need help. Your family could **volunteer** to serve food at a soup kitchen. You could also gather canned goods, used clothes, blankets, and toys to donate, or give, to people in need.

## Serve the Earth

You can serve your neighborhood community by serving Earth. Neighborhoods need green spaces. Find out if you could plant a tree in a park or build a community garden. You could also put a bird feeder in your own yard or grow flowers there.

## How to Be a Good Neighbor

What does it mean to be a good member of your neighborhood community? It means taking part. It means working toward making your neighborhood the very best it can be. Your actions make a difference. Get started today!

# GLOSSARY

**achieve:** to get by effort

**citizen:** someone who lives in a country legally and has certain rights

**collector:** a person who collects things, such as trash, for their job

**goal:** something important someone wants to do

**ordinary:** normal, not unusual or special

**productive:** getting good results from working hard

**volunteer:** to work without pay

# FOR MORE INFORMATION

## BOOKS

Andres, Marco. *Community Service and Volunteering*. New York, NY: PowerKids Press, 2018.

Nagle, Jeanne. *What Is a Community?* New York, NY: Britannica, 2018.

## WEBSITES

**Kid World Citizen**
*kidworldcitizen.org/35-service-projects-for-kids/*
Discover more fun community service projects.

**Start a Snowball**
*startasnowball.com/kids-service-project-ideas-2/*
Brainstorm new ways to pitch in in your neighborhood.

# INDEX